Petra Boase's Super

Stamp Factory

southwater

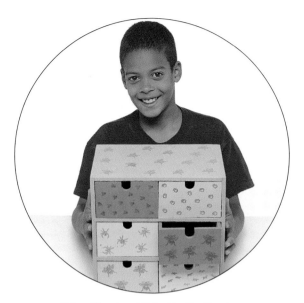

This edition is published by Southwater

Southwater is an imprint of Anness Publishing Ltd
Hermes House, 88–89 Blackfriars Road, London SE1 8HA
tel. 020 7401 2077; fax 020 7633 9499
www.southwaterbooks.com; info@anness.com

© Anness Publishing Ltd 1996, 2003

This edition distributed in the UK by The Manning Partnership Ltd,
6 The Old Dairy, Melcombe Road, Bath BA2 3LR;
tel. 01225 478 444; fax 01225 478 440;
sales@manning-partnership.co.uk

This edition distributed in the USA and Canada by National Book
Network, 4720 Boston Way, Lanham, MD 20706;
tel. 301 459 3366; fax 301 459 1705;
www.nbnbooks.com

This edition distributed in Australia by Pan Macmillan Australia,
Level 18, St Martins Tower, 31 Market St, Sydney, NSW 2000;
tel. 1300 135 113; fax 1300 135 103;
email customer.service@macmillan.com.au

This edition distributed in New Zealand by The Five Mile Press (NZ)
Ltd, PO Box 33–1071 Takapuna, Unit 11/
101–111 Diana Drive, Glenfield, Auckland 10;
tel. (09) 444 4144; fax (09) 444 4518; fivemilenz@clear.net.nz

A CIP catalogue record for this book is available from the British Library.

Publisher: Joanna Lorenz
Senior Children's Books Editor: Caroline Beattie
Assistant Editor: Sophie Warne
Photographer: John Freeman
Designers: Tony Sambrook and Edward Kinsey

13 5 7 9 10 8 6 4 2

Introduction

Stamping is a very creative form of decoration and is great fun to do. If you are unable to buy any ready-made rubber stamps, don't panic. On pages 9–11 we show you how to make your very own stamps, using all sorts of different materials, which you will probably find lying around your home.

The projects in this book are very exciting, and I'm sure that after reading only a few of them you will be eager to get to work. However, before you do, it is very important to organize yourself. Make sure that you have covered the surface you are working on with an old cloth or with newspaper, and that all the equipment you need is close at hand.

Whether you are using ready-made rubber stamps or your home-made ones, remember to wash them gently after use and before you switch to different colored ink. Dry them gently with a towel. Also never forget to put the lids on the printing inks, otherwise they might dry up. However, the important thing about stamping is to let your imagination run wild and to have lots and lots of fun!

Petra Boase

Contents

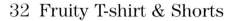

Materials & Equipment

Fabric ink pens

Fabric paint

Pigment ink pads

STAMPS WITH HANDLES

These are great if you want to get a firm hold of the stamp when you are using it to print.

WOODEN BLOCK STAMPS

These are the heaviest stamps and they feel very stable when you print with them.

ROLLER STAMPS

These are long rubber stamps that are on a roller. You roll them first on the ink pad and then roll it over the surface on which you want to print. The print will be in a line. The longer you want the print to be, the more ink you have to apply to the stamp.

RUBBER STAMPS (PART OF A KIT)

This is probably the cheapest way to buy rubber stamps. The kits usually have a theme, for example, sea life, and within the kit you get lots of different stamps.

FABRIC INK STAMP PAD

This is a fabric pad and you pour the fabric ink onto it. When the ink runs out you simply add more ink. You will need a separate pad for each different colored ink.

FABRIC PAINT OR STAMPING INK

This comes in a bottle and you pour it onto a fabric stamp pad. Always make sure the lid is screwed on tightly so that if it falls over it won't leak and make a mess.

FABRIC INK PENS

These look like felt-tipped pens. You simply color the stamp using a mixture of colors and then print on to fabric. Remember to put the lids on after use, otherwise they will dry up.

PRINTING FELT PENS

These also look like felt-tipped pens. You can color the rubber stamp, using as many colors as you like, and then print on to paper or card. Remember to put the lids on after use.

INK PADS

These come in an assortment of colors and are used to color stamps for printing on paper and card.

PIGMENT INK PADS

These use a different kind of ink, and their colors are very strong and bright. Use on card, paper, and wood.

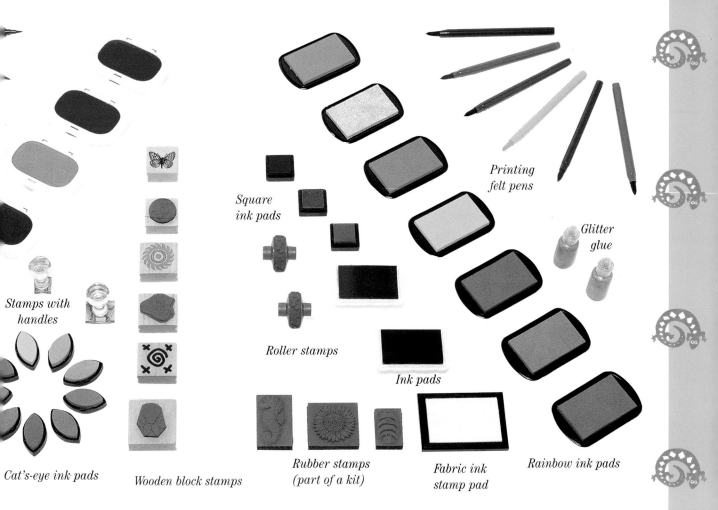

Stamps with handles

Square ink pads

Printing felt pens

Glitter glue

Roller stamps

Ink pads

Cat's-eye ink pads

Wooden block stamps

Rubber stamps (part of a kit)

Fabric ink stamp pad

Rainbow ink pads

RAINBOW INK PADS
These are ink pads with several inks in them. When you print the stamp, the print will be multicolored.

CAT'S-EYE INK PADS
Use an assortment of colors and dab them onto the rubber stamp to create a multicolored print.

SQUARE INK PADS
These are good if you only have very small rubber stamps. They are also useful if you want to dab different colors on to the stamp to create a multicolored print.

GLITTER GLUE
This is great for decorating your stamped prints, but allow the glue to dry thoroughly before touching it or else it will smudge.

7

Creative Ideas

Rubber stamps come in all shapes and sizes and in an enormous range of images and patterns. These are a few examples of different effects you can get from different colors and patterns. A pigment ink stamp pad was used for all the prints here.

1 Use a roller stamp to decorate a ribbon for a present or even to put in your hair.

2 You can use an ordinary stamp to give the same effect as a roller, by printing the motif several times in a row.

3 Repeat a motif several times in rows to give a neat pattern.

4 Repeat a motif in a more scattered way to give a freer pattern.

6 Use colors that are quite close to each other to give a subtle print.

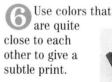

7 Use contrasting inks and papers to give a very bright effect.

5 Experiment with different-colored inks and papers. Pink ink on blue paper could give you a purple print, whereas blue ink on pink paper could still give you a blue print.

8

Home-Made Stamps

Making your own stamps means that you get your very own unique motifs.

SAFETY FIRST!

To make some home-made stamps, the shape needs to be cut out with a craft knife – ALWAYS ask an adult to do this for you.

STRING

1 Cut out a square of cardboard. Paint glue over the card and, starting in the center, begin to coil a length of string into a spiral shape. Cut the end of the string when you have made your shape.

2 Paint the string with paint (or with fabric paint) and print, pressing down firmly. You will need to re-apply the paint onto the string for each print. String gives you designs with nice fine lines.

CORD

1 If you want a chunky, textured effect, then use cord. Cut out a square of cardboard. Measure and cut a piece of cord and glue it in a circle on the card. Glue a shorter length of cord in a circle in the middle of the other circle. Leave the glue to harden.

2 Paint the cord with paint or, if you are printing onto fabric, with fabric paint, and print, pressing down firmly. You will need to re-apply paint onto the cord for each print. Don't put too much paint on the cord, so that the design is nice and clear.

CARDBOARD

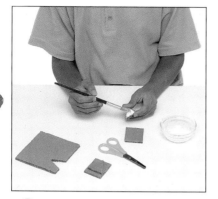  

1 Cut a piece of cardboard into a square. Cut another piece of cardboard into whatever shape you want and glue it onto the square. Allow the glue to harden.

2 Stamp the card shape onto a pigment ink pad and print, pressing firmly. If you are printing on fabric, use a fabric ink pad. Re-apply the ink after each print.

ERASER

1 Draw a shape on one side of an eraser with a ballpoint pen or a pencil. Ask an adult to cut down into the rubber around the shape with a craft knife, cutting the extra parts of the eraser away to leave the shape you want.

2 Stamp the eraser on an ink pad and print. Using an eraser to make a stamp gives a smooth finish, like a store-bought rubber stamp.

10

SPONGE

1 Draw a shape on the sponge with a felt pen. Ask an adult to cut around the shape with a craft knife, cutting the extra sponge away.

2 Dab the sponge on a plate of paint or fabric paint. Sponge stamps give a varied texture to your motif. Wash the sponge after use.

POTATO

1 Cut a potato in half and draw a shape on one half with a felt-tipped pen. Ask an adult to cut away the potato outside your shape with a knife.

2 Stamp the potato on an ink pad and print. If you are printing on fabric, remember to use a fabric ink pad.

Creating a Picture

You can create a picture in several different ways: you can print lots of different motifs to build up a scene, you can repeat stamps to give a pattern, or you can give the same stamp different colors.

1 Use a selection of different stamps and colors to create a picture or story. This picture is all about sea life. You could even write your own story alongside the picture you have created.

2 A repeat pattern can either be very compact, like these bones, or very spacious. You can also experiment with using more than one image.

3 If you are worried about printing in a straight line, simply draw a straight line with a ruler and a pencil. This will act as a good guideline and, when your stamping has dried, you can erase the pencil marks.

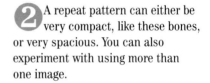

4 You will be amazed at how many different effects you can make from one stamp. For a really colorful effect, you can print the same motif in different inks on different papers, then cut them out carefully and arrange them on a card.

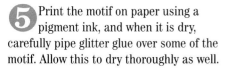

5 Print the motif on paper using a pigment ink, and when it is dry, carefully pipe glitter glue over some of the motif. Allow this to dry thoroughly as well.

6 If you use pigment ink by itself, use colors that you really like. Choose the color of the paper carefully, and experiment with different ink colors to create your favorite combinations.

7 A rainbow ink pad gives your stamp several different colors at once. Make sure they will all show up on the paper you choose.

8 With printing felt-tipped pens you can color different parts of the stamp. This stamp was colored red and green before printing, but the black seeds were filled in later.

13

Paw Print Paper

Create your own designer wrapping paper and matching ribbon to make presents you wrap look extra special.

YOU WILL NEED

Paper
Pigment ink pads
Paw print stamp
Ribbon
Adhesive tape
Scissors
Scottie dog
  roller stamp

1 Take a large piece of colored paper and lay it on a smooth flat surface. Cover the paper with stamped paw prints. You could do these in rows or at random.

2 Lay the ribbon out on a flat surface. Stick one end down with a piece of tape. Smooth the ribbon out, then tape down the other end.

3 Roll the roller stamp on the ink pad, then carefully roll it along the ribbon. To cover a long piece of ribbon, you will need to re-ink the stamp. Try to match up the design as carefully as possible each time.

4 When the ink has dried on the paper and ribbon, you are ready to wrap your present. Tie the ribbon around the parcel and finish with a bow.

Fishy Folders

Give an ordinary file or folder a new look with the following ideas. If your folder is old and tattered, cover it with a fresh piece of paper before you begin. The pocket on the front of this folder is very useful for storing pens and pencils in.

1 Cut a piece of colored posterboard into a rectangle and paint a line of glue along two long sides and a short side. Glue the pocket to the front of the file and press down gently to make sure it sticks and holds in place.

2 Cut a piece of fringe to fit along the open edge of the pocket and glue it on. You can make your own fringe by cutting into a strip of paper.

3 Cut out lots of paper fish shapes and print fish stamps on them. When the ink is dry, glue the shapes to the file.

4 You could also glue some cut-out paper fish to a paper folder, then print shells around them.

17

Pom-pom Pencil Pot

Transform a plastic bottle into a container for anything from pencils to wooden spoons. If you have lots of plastic bottles, you could make a set and cover them with different colored papers.

YOU WILL NEED
Plastic bottle
Tape measure
Craft knife
Scissors
Construction paper
Dalmatian dog stamp
Pigment ink pad
Double-sided adhesive tape
Pom-pom braid
Glue

1 Draw a straight line around a plastic bottle (at the same height all the way round). Ask an adult to cut it for you. Keep the bottom half.

2 Measure the height of the bottle and then measure around it with a tape measure. Cut a piece of paper to the same height and width of the bottle, but add $1/4$ in to the width to give an overlap. Lay the paper on a smooth flat surface and print all over it. Let the ink dry.

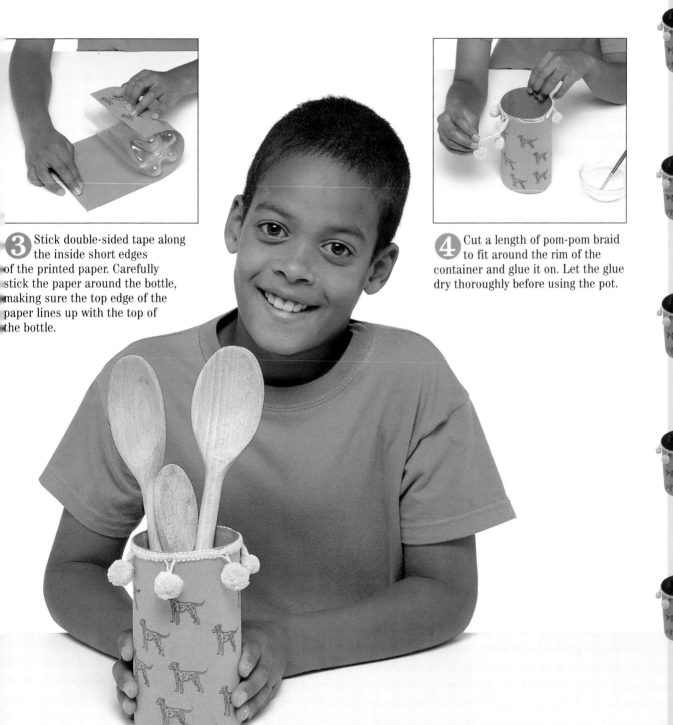

Stick double-sided tape along the inside short edges of the printed paper. Carefully stick the paper around the bottle, making sure the top edge of the paper lines up with the top of the bottle.

Cut a length of pom-pom braid to fit around the rim of the container and glue it on. Let the glue dry thoroughly before using the pot.

Starry Pillowcase

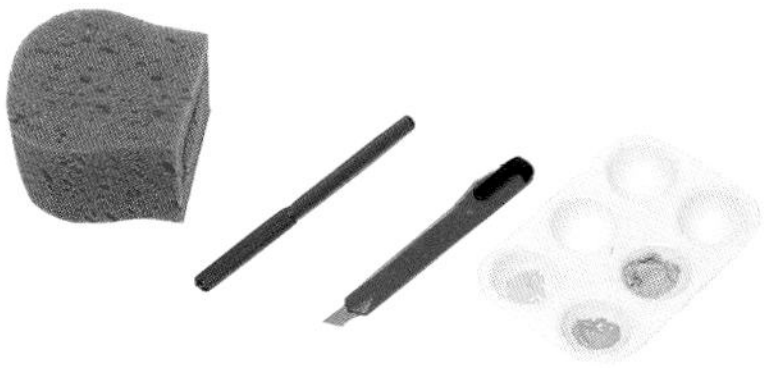

Turn your skills to a bit of textile printing and re-design your pillowcase. If you are feeling adventurous, why not decorate your sheets to match your pillowcase?

YOU WILL NEED

Sponge
Felt-tipped pen
Craft knife
Scrap paper
Plain pillowcase
Fabric paint
Old plate
Iron

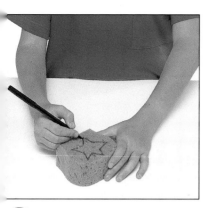

1 Draw a star on a smooth sponge with a felt pen.

2 Ask an adult to cut around the star using a craft knife. Keep the leftover pieces of sponge: they might come in useful for making another sponge stamp.

3 Place a scrap piece of paper inside the pillowcase and lay it on a flat, smooth surface. Pour some fabric paint onto an old plate and dab the sponge in it. Press the sponge gently on the pillowcase to make a print. Re-apply the paint to the sponge for each print.

4 When you have covered the first side of the pillowcase with your prints, leave it to dry thoroughly. Turn the pillowcase over and do the same to the other side. When the pillowcase is finished and the paint is completely dry, ask an adult to iron over the design to set the paint.

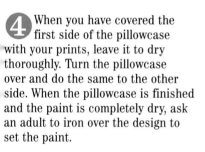

Covered Boxes

This project shows you how to jazz up cardboard boxes. Recycle boxes by covering them with decorated paper. They're terrific for storing all your bits and pieces in.

YOU WILL NEED
Colored paper
Scissors
Pig stamp
Chicken stamp
Pigment ink pads
Boxes to recycle
Glue

1 Cut out circles of paper in lots of bright colors.

2 Stamp each circle with the pig or chicken stamp, using brightly colored inks that contrast with the paper. Leave the ink to dry.

3 Arrange the circles where you want them before glueing them to your box.

4 You can also completely cover lots of different boxes with colored paper and then print onto the paper.

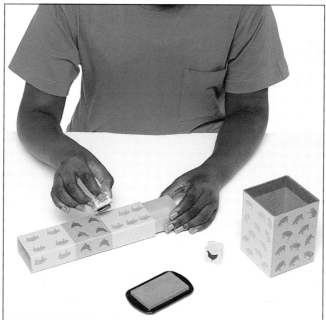

Lovely Letters

Your friends will enjoy reading a letter from you even more if it's on stylish designer paper.

YOU WILL NEED

Envelope
Colored paper
Ruler and pencil
Glue
Scissors
Rocket stamp
Pigment ink pads
Globe stamp
Cat's-eye ink pads
White stickers

1 If you're not sure how to make an envelope, simply take one that hasn't been used and open the seams. Place it on a colored piece of paper and draw around it. Fold it in the right places and glue the sides to hold it together, but leave the top flap open. Decorate the front of the envelope with stamp prints, too, if you want.

2 Cut out a piece of writing paper from colored paper, making it the same width as the envelope and twice as long. Lay it on a smooth flat surface. Decorate around the edge of the paper with stamps to match the envelopes. Allow the ink to dry.

3 Use the cat's-eye ink pads to color the globe stamp and then print onto a plain white sticker. For each print you will need to re-apply the ink.

4 When the ink has dried, cut around the globe and use it to seal the envelope after you have written your letter.

*F*lower *C*ards & *T*ags

Friends and family are always delighted to receive a home-made card or gift tag on their present. Why not print the same design you print on the cards onto a piece of colored paper to make matching wrapping paper?

YOU WILL NEED

Sunflower stamp
Pigment ink pads
Colored paper
Scissors
Glue
Ruler
Hole punch
Ribbon

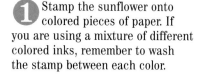

1 Stamp the sunflower onto colored pieces of paper. If you are using a mixture of different colored inks, remember to wash the stamp between each color.

2 Cut around the sunflower and glue it onto a colorful luggage label. You can make your own label out of card. Punch a hole at the top of the gift tag with a hole punch.

3 To make a greeting card, fold a piece of colored paper in half and glue a sunflower to the front. See how creative you can be by making as many different cards and gift tags as possible.

4 To thread the ribbon through the gift tag hole, fold the ribbon in half, push the folded end through the hole, then pull the other end through the loop. Tie or stick it onto your present.

Rocket & Star Pot

If you are unable to find a terracotta flowerpot at home, you can buy one from most gardening stores and hardware stores. This project shows how you can turn the flowerpot into a designer container for your odds and ends or for a plant.

YOU WILL NEED

Terracotta flowerpot
Acrylic or latex paint
Paintbrush
Rocket stamp
Pigment ink pads
Home-made rubber stamp
Varnish

1 Cover the surface you are working on with newspaper or an old cloth to avoid making a mess. Paint the outside of the pot (except the rim) a bright color. Leave the paint to dry thoroughly.

2 Paint the inside of the pot and the rim in a contrasting color to the outside. Leave the paint to dry again.

3 With a very steady hand, print the rocket around the rim of the pot, being careful not to slip. You might want to ask an adult or a friend to hold the pot for you.

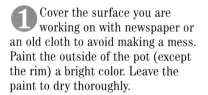

4 Cut a home-made rubber stamp into the shape of a star, and use it to print on the outside of the pot. Leave the ink to dry thoroughly and then varnish the pot. It is important to do this if you are going to put a plant in the pot.

Fringed Party Cups

Drinking out of these fun cups will
cause great excitement at your party!

YOU WILL NEED

Plastic or paper cups
Colored paper
Ruler
Scissors
Cow roller stamp
Pigment ink pads
Double-sided adhesive tape

1 Measure and cut out a strip of colorful paper for the fringe, long enough to fit around the plastic cups and 2 in deep.

2 Roll the stamp on the ink pad, then roll it along one edge of the strip of paper. Let the ink dry.

3 Cut a fringe along the other edge of the paper by making evenly spaced cuts that are the same length. Do not cut into the stamps.

4 Stick a strip of double-sided tape on the back of the paper behind the row of cows. Then carefully stick the paper fringe around the rim of the cup. You might need the help of an adult or a friend to hold the cup steady while you do this.

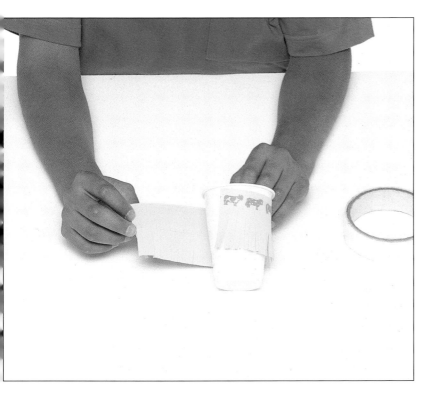

Fruity T-shirt & Shorts

This outfit is perfect for the summer when the sun is shining and it's nice and warm outdoors. Your friends will be so impressed by your new outfit they will be wondering where you bought it!

YOU WILL NEED

T-shirt
Old paper
Fabric paint or stamping inks
Fabric ink pads
Strawberry stamp
Watermelon stamp
Shorts
Iron

1 Lay the T-shirt flat on a covered work surface with a piece of paper inside it. This will prevent the print going through to the other side of the T-shirt and making a mess.

2 Using fabric ink, print strawberries all over the front of the T-shirt. Print watermelons in the spaces between the strawberries. Allow the inks to dry thoroughly before trying on the T-shirt.

3 Place your shorts flat on the work surface and print strawberries around the legs. Remember to re-ink the stamp so that the strawberries look the same.

4 When the ink has dried on both the T-shirt and shorts, ask an adult to iron them for you (with a paper towel under the iron) to set the ink.

33

Polka-dot Pillow Cover

Add some color to a plain pillow cover by painting lots of polka-dots on it and printing on top of them with a potato print.

Potato
Knife
Felt pen
Pillow cover
Newspaper
Fabric paint
Paintbrush
Fabric inks
Fabric ink pads
Iron

1 Ask an adult to cut a potato in half, and with a felt-tipped pen draw a circle on one half of the potato. Then ask an adult to cut around the circle with a knife.

2 Cover the surface you are working on with newspaper and lay the pillow cover flat. Place a piece of newspaper inside the cushion cover to separate the two sides. Paint large circles on the fabric. Leave the paint to dry.

3 Dab the potato on the ink pad and print onto the painted circles. Do this to all the circles.

4 When the ink is completely dry, ask an adult to iron over the polka-dots to set the ink and paint.

Sea Frieze

Decorate a wall with this magical frieze full of exciting sea life. Ask an adult before you start the project, just in case they want to help you.

YOU WILL NEED

Colored paper squares
Large piece of card
Glue
Pigment ink pads
Shell stamps
Seaweed stamps
Fish stamps
Octopus stamp

1 Stick the colored squares of paper next to each other along a wall or on a length of cardboard. Make sure the ends join up neatly.

2 Starting with the shell stamps, print along the bottom edge of the squares. It is a good idea to stand back from your work every so often so you can see how the story is progressing and to check that you are printing in the right place.

3 Print the seaweed stamp along the squares above the shells. Print over some of the joins between the colored squares.

4 Print the fish and other creatures in between the seaweed and the shells. Leave the inks to dry thoroughly before touching the frieze.

37

Gift Bag

This bag is a fun way of wrapping up a gift for someone you love! Change the size of the bag to match the present, but make sure your present isn't too heavy, otherwise it might break the bag.

YOU WILL NEED

Colored paper
Ruler
Scissors
Glue
Hole punch
Ribbon
Strawberry stamp
Printing felt-tipped pens

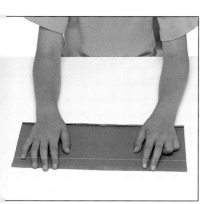

1 Measure and cut out a piece of paper 12 by 5¹/₂ in. Fold the paper in half and open it out again. Fold over each long side by ¹/₄ in.

2 Paint a line of glue along the folded edges. Fold the paper in half, pressing the sides firmly so that they stick together.

3 Punch two holes through the top of the bag about 2 in apart from each other. Cut two lengths of ribbon 8 in long and thread each one through a set of the punched holes, tying a knot at the ends to keep them secure.

4 To make rubber stamps print in different colors, use the printing felt-tipped pens to color the leaves green and the strawberry red. Stamp the strawberry onto a piece of paper. You will need to re-color the strawberry stamp for each print. Cut out the strawberries and glue them onto the bag.

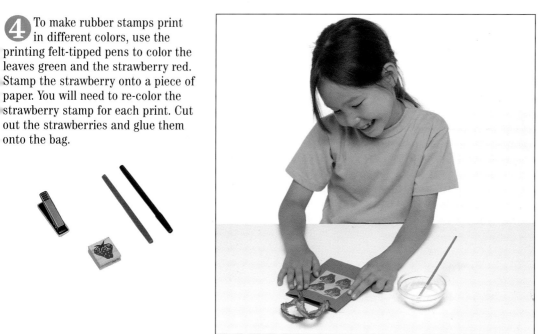

Party Napkins

Decorate your party table with your own designer paper napkins. Why not stamp each napkin in a different style for each friend?

YOU WILL NEED
Plain colored party napkins
Scissors
Dragon stamp
Pig stamp
Star stamp
Pigment ink pads

1 Decorate some of the napkins by snipping a fringe around the edge. Be careful if you are using sharp scissors.

2 On the other napkins cut zigzags or spikes around the edges. Make sure they are even.

3 Lay each napkin on a smooth, flat, covered surface and stamp a row around the edges. Make sure the stamps are evenly spaced and that they are level with each other.

4 Fill in the center with different stamped prints in your own design. Let each napkin dry thoroughly before you lay them on your party table.

41

Flower Power Leggings

Decorate a plain pair of leggings with lots of different flowers. You can use colors that blend in or contrasting colors that match a T-shirt.

YOU WILL NEED

Plain colored leggings
Scrap paper
Set of flower stamps
Fabric ink
Fabric ink pads
Iron

1 Cover the surface you are working on with paper. Lay the leggings flat on the surface. Cut a piece of paper to fit up inside each leg and at the top.

2 Using fabric ink, print flowers on the leggings. Print all over the fabric, since when you have the leggings on they will stretch and the stamps will spread out a little.

3 Print some leaves in a contrasting color between the flowers. Leave the ink to dry.

4 Ask an adult to iron over the flowers to set the ink. After that the leggings are ready to wear!

Bug Socks

Shock your friends with these creepy-crawly socks. Remember to use cotton socks so that you can iron them to set the ink.

YOU WILL NEED

Plain colored cotton socks
Bug stamps
Fabric ink
Fabric ink pad
Iron

1 Cover the surface you are working on with paper or an old cloth and lay the sock flat. Print the spider all over the socks.

2 Print the smaller bugs around the spiders. When the ink has dried, turn the socks over and do the same to the other side.

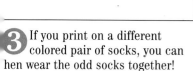

3 If you print on a different colored pair of socks, you can then wear the odd socks together!

4 When the ink has dried thoroughly, ask an adult to iron each sock under a paper towel to set the ink, otherwise the bugs might crawl off!

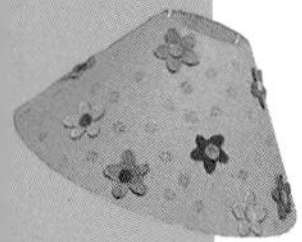

Blossoming Lamp Shade

Make bedtime reading fun by decorating your bedside lamp. Be very gentle when you are printing onto a lamp shade, as the surface isn't very firm and you don't want to slip and smudge your design.

YOU WILL NEED

Pen
Felt
Scissors
Glue
Lamp shade
Flower stamp
Fabric inks
Fabric ink pads
Paintbrush and paints

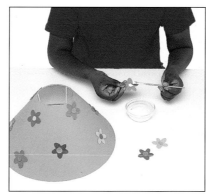

1 Draw flower shapes on pieces of felt and cut them out. Cut out contrasting circles for the centers and glue them on the flowers.

2 Glue the felt flowers onto the lamp shade, pressing them on with one hand and holding the back of the lamp shade with the other.

3 Carefully apply the flower stamp to the lamp shade, in between the felt flowers, using a variety of colored inks.

4 If your lamp shade has a base, you could paint it a bright color to match the flowers or paint stripes on it. Allow it to dry before attaching the lamp shade to it. Ask an adult to help you screw in a bulb before you plug it in and light up!

Waste Basket

If you think this watermelon waste basket looks too good to put your garbage in, you could store your bits and pieces in it.

YOU WILL NEED

Colored paper
Watermelon stamp
Pigment ink pads
Scissors
Plain square waste paper basket
Paintbrush and paints
Glue
Home-made rubber stamp

  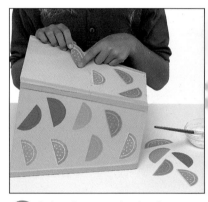

1 Stamp watermelon shapes onto different colored paper using an assortment of colored inks. Remember to wipe the melon clean between each new color.

2 When the ink has dried, cut around the printed melons.

3 Paint the waste basket in one color, and paint the corners in a contrasting color. When the paint has dried, glue the melon shapes onto the basket and leave to dry.

4 Using a home-made stamp made from an eraser, stamp the inside of the bin. If your waste basket is metal this will not work, so print the shape onto pieces of paper first and then glue them on.

Stamped Scarf

You can wear this fun scarf around your neck or in your hair. You could make your own scarf to print on by cutting out a square piece of plain fabric, folding over the edges and sewing them down.

YOU WILL NEED

*Large white scarf or
    piece of fabric
Different motif stamps
Fabric inks
Fabric ink pads
Iron*

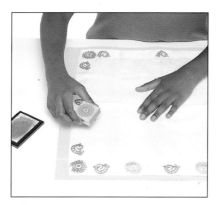

1 Cover the surface you are working on with an old cloth or a piece of newspaper. Spread the scarf flat on the surface and stamp the same image in the four corners of the scarf.

2 Using different colored inks, stamp different motifs around the edge of the scarf.

3 Scatter more motifs in different colors in the middle of the scarf, and leave the inks to dry.

4 When the inks have dried, place an old piece of cloth on an ironing board and place the scarf on top of it with the right side facing down. Ask an adult to iron it all over and this will set the inks.

5 When you choose the ink colors for your stamps, try to match them to some clothes you already have so that you can team up your new scarf with your wardrobe.

Butterfly Pencil Case

Make your very own pencil case using pieces of felt. If you dislike sewing you could always use fabric glue to hold the sides together and sticky pieces of Velcro to fasten the pencil case.

YOU WILL NEED

Square of felt
Needle
Thread
Fabric glue
Snaps
Scraps of colored felt
  Butterfly stamp
    Fabric ink
    Fabric ink pad

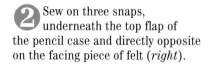

1 Fold the square of felt as shown in the photograph and sew along each side using a simple running stitch, or carefully glue a strip down the sides with fabric glue.

2 Sew on three snaps, underneath the top flap of the pencil case and directly opposite on the facing piece of felt (*right*).

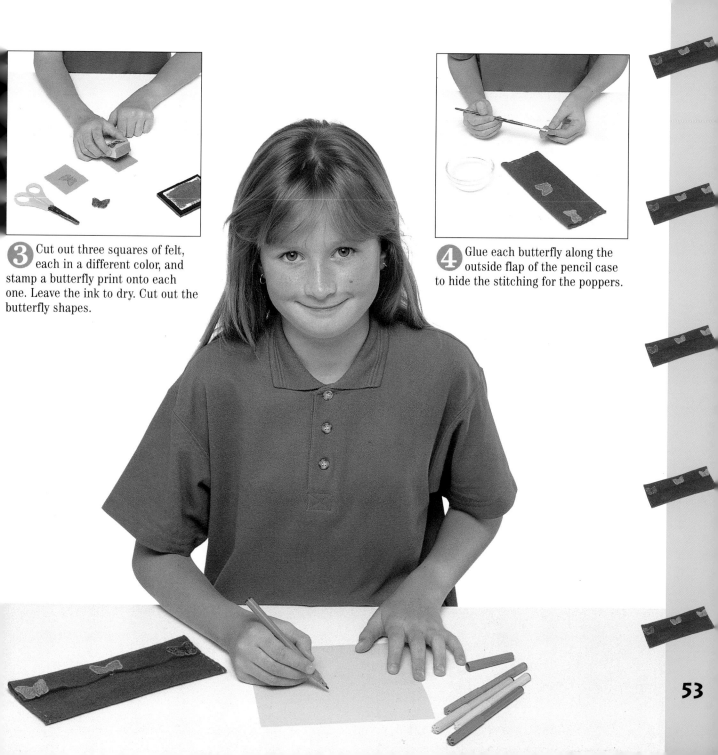

3 Cut out three squares of felt, each in a different color, and stamp a butterfly print onto each one. Leave the ink to dry. Cut out the butterfly shapes.

4 Glue each butterfly along the outside flap of the pencil case to hide the stitching for the poppers.

Beastie Drawers

If you have an old cupboard or small piece of furniture, why not give it a lick of paint and stamp some fun images onto it? Remember that painting can be messy, so cover the surface you are working on with lots of newspaper or an old cloth.

YOU WILL NEED

Set of small drawers
Latex paints
Paintbrush
Set of bug stamps
Bumblebee stamp
Pigment ink pads

1 If you are painting a small chest of drawers, remove the drawers from the frame. Paint the frame a bright color and let the paint dry thoroughly. You might need to put on two coats of paint. Ask an adult for advice.

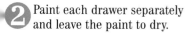

2 Paint each drawer separately and leave the paint to dry.

3 When the drawers have dried, put them back in the frame. On each drawer's front print a different collection of bugs.

4 Print the bumblebee stamp around the frame of the chest of drawers. Allow the inks to dry before you put all your bits and pieces back in the drawers.

Doodle Sneakers

Give a pair of sneakers a new look by printing fun patterns all over them. You could also replace the plain shoelaces with bright pieces of ribbon to add an extra splash of color.

YOU WILL NEED

Plain colored cotton sneakers
Newspaper
Set of doodle stamps
Fabric inks
Fabric stamp pads
Fabric glitter glue
Ribbon

1 Fill each sneaker with scrunched-up newspaper. Press it in quite firmly. This will make the sneakers easier to print on.

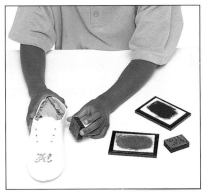

2 Print the doodle stamps on the sneakers, pressing very gently. It might help if you slip one hand in behind the spot where you want to stamp. Leave the ink to dry.

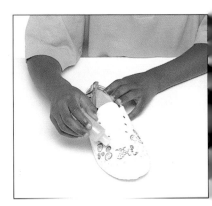

3 Decorate the sneakers with fabric glitter glue in funny shapes or small spots; allow to set.

4 Thread a brightly colored piece of ribbon through the lace holes of each sneaker. They are now ready to try on and dance around in.

Cactus Dish Towel

This dish towel will definitely spice up the kitchen, and it makes a great present.

YOU WILL NEED

Plain dish towel
Cactus stamps
Fabric inks
Fabric ink pads
Chili pepper stamp
Iron

1 Lay the dish towel flat on a well-covered surface and print one kind of cactus around the edges with a 4 in gap between each print.

2 Using a different cactus stamp, print in between the shapes you have just printed around the edges of the dish towel.

3 Scatter-print chili peppers in the middle of the dish towel. Allow the inks to dry thoroughly.

4 When the inks have dried, lay an old piece of cloth on the ironing board and place the dish towel with the design facing down. Ask an adult to iron over the design for you so that the inks set.

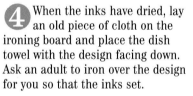

59

Swirly Bag

This project shows you how to make a rope print block. As well as using this bag for laundry, you could use it for your sports clothes or as a vacation bag.

YOU WILL NEED

Posterboard
Scissors
Cotton cord
Glue
Pillowcase
Needle
Thread
Old paper
Paintbrush
Fabric paint
Ribbon
Safety pin

1 Cut a piece of posterboard in a square. Cut a length of cord and glue it in a circle onto the card, holding it down until it feels secure. Cut a small strip of posterboard and fold it in half. Glue one half onto the print block to form a handle.

2 With the pillowcase right side out, fold over the opening edge by 2 in and sew it down all around with a line of running stitches.

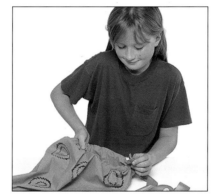

③ Place a piece of paper inside the pillowcase to separate the two sides and lay it on a flat surface. Paint the cord stamp with fabric paint and press it down firmly on the fabric. You will need to re-apply the paint onto the cord for each print. When you have covered the fabric with the prints, leave the paint to dry and then print on the other side.

④ Cut a length of ribbon about three times the width of the pillowcase. Pin the safety pin to one end of it. Snip a hole in the tube you have sewn around the opening of the pillowcase and thread the ribbon through it. Tie the two ends in a knot and pull the ribbon to close the bag.

Flowery **F**rame

You can put a photograph
of your favorite animal or
friend or a piece of your
artwork in this fun frame
and hang it on your
bedroom wall.

YOU WILL NEED

Posterboard
Ruler
Scissors
Craft knife
  Colored paper
  Glue
    Butterfly stamp
    Pigment ink pad
     Adhesive tape
      Ribbon

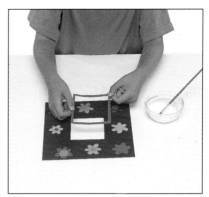

1 Using a ruler, measure a piece of card 8 in by 8 in and cut it out. Measure a square 3 in by 3 in in the center of the frame and ask an adult to cut it out with a craft knife.

2 Draw flowers on different colored paper, and cut them out. Cut circles for the centers of the flowers and glue them on.

3 Glue the flowers onto the frame. Ask an adult to cut a thin frame of colored paper to go around the hole in the center of the frame. Glue it on carefully.

4 Stamp the butterfly shapes around the frame, between the flowers and leave the ink to dry.

5 Cut out a square piece of card 4 in by 4 in and tape it to the back of the frame, leaving one edge open to put the photograph or picture in. Cut a short piece of ribbon and fold it in half. Tape it to the top edge of the frame and hang the finished picture on the wall.

ACKNOWLEDGEMENTS

The Publishers would like to thank the following manufacturers for providing the rubber stamps and other materials for this book:

First Class Stamps:
Fish (pages 16–17 and 36–37), seaweed (pages 36–37), flowers (pages 42–43 and 46–47), doodles (pages 56–57).

Inca Stamp:
Paw print (pages 14–15), shell (pages 16–17), pig and chicken (pages 22–23), globe (pages 24–25), sunflower (pages 26–27), octopus, shell, group of shells (pages 36–37), and bumblebee (pages 54–55).

Make Your Mark:
Dalmatian (pages 18–19), rocket (pages 24–25 and 28–29), dragon and pig (pages 40–41), butterfly (pages 62–63).

Rubber Stampede:
Scottie dog roller stamp (pages 14–15), cow roller stamp (pages 30–31), Watermelon and strawberry (pages 32–33, 38–39 and 48–49), bug (pages 44–45 and 54–55), motifs (pages 50–51), butterfly (pages 52–53), chilies and cacti (pages 58–59).

The Publishers would also like to thank the following children (and their parents!) for modeling for this book:

Kristina Chase, Leoni Hughes-Brown, Lana Green, Lee Johnson, Reece Johnson, Janel Kiamil, Mai-Anh Peterson, Alexandra Richards, Leigh Richards.